BRIGHT
IDEA
BOOKS

THE World
WAS ONCE
COVERED BY
Giant Mushrooms:
COOL EARTH FACTS

by Kimberly M. Hutmacher

raintree

a Capstone company — publishers for children

Raintree is an imprint of Capstone Global Library Limited, a company incorporated in England and Wales having its registered office at 264 Banbury Road, Oxford, OX2 7DY – Registered company number: 6695582

www.raintree.co.uk
myorders@raintree.co.uk

Edited by Meg Gaertner
Designed by Becky Daum
Production by Colleen McLaren
Printed and bound in India

ISBN 978 1 4747 7458 1 (hardback)
ISBN 978 1 4747 8243 2 (paperback)

British Library Cataloguing in Publication Data
A full catalogue record for this book is available from the British Library.

Acknowledgements
We would like to thank the following for permission to reproduce photographs: iStockphoto: DHuss, 18–19, GomezDavid, 21, Harvepino, 11, miljko, cover, mrtom-uk, 8–9, red_moon_rise, 14–15, shauni, 7, Spondylolithesis, 9, sreenath_k, 22–23, vjanez, cover, Wicki58, 12; Shutterstock Images: chuyuss, 25, Fotos593, 30–31, mTaira, 5, NatureDiver, romvo, cover, sunsinger, 26–27, TommoT, 24, Yai, 17
Every effort has been made to contact copyright holders of material reproduced in this book. Any omissions will be rectified in subsequent printings if notice is given to the publisher.

We would like to thank Gabi Laske, PhD, for her help with this book.

CONTENTS

AMAZING
Earth

Volcanoes erupt. Some bury cities. **Earthquakes** send waves across the ocean. Huge mushrooms give way to trees. Earth changes over time. Our planet is amazing!

The storm waves
caused by some
earthquakes can
destroy houses.

HURTLING
Through
Space

Earth spins once a day. It moves fastest at the **equator**. It spins at about 1,600 kilometres (1,000 miles) per hour. The speed never changes. People do not feel Earth moving. They move with it.

6

EARTH'S PATH

Earth **orbits** the Sun each year. It travels 107,800 km (67,000 miles) per hour.

Taking a photo over a long time catches what seems to be the movement of stars. But it is actually the Earth that is spinning.

The Sun gives off solar wind, a stream of particles that spreads through space.

SPINNING MAGNET

Earth is a big **magnet**. It has an iron core. The core makes a magnetic field. The field protects the Earth. It blocks harmful **particles** from the Sun. It also guides bird **migration**.

Birds use the magnetic field to know which direction they should fly during migration.

CHAPTER 3

LONG, LONG Ago

Earth has seven continents today. But the continents are always moving. They come together. They break apart. Earth has had only one continent at times. Pangaea was the most recent giant continent. It broke apart 200 million years ago.

North America moves about 2.3 centimetres (1 inch) each year.

Scientists learn about the past by studying the remains of plants and animals.

THE GREAT DYING

Earth has seen many mass **extinctions**. One of them happened on Pangaea. It was the Permian extinction. It killed off 96 per cent of **species**. The other 4 per cent lived. They **evolved**. Today's life comes from that 4 per cent.

GOODBYE DINOS

The K–T extinction was 66 million years ago. It killed off the dinosaurs.

GIANT MUSHROOMS

A huge **fungus** once covered Earth. This was 420 to 350 million years ago. Mushrooms grew taller than today's giraffes! Today the largest organism is a fungus. It is in Oregon, USA. It would cover more than 1,800 football pitches. It is mostly underground. But it shoots out of the soil in places. There, people can see its mushrooms.

A mushroom is
a type of fungus.

CHAPTER 4
RUMBLING
Giant

The Earth is active. Giant plates underground move. Their motion can cause earthquakes. The strongest one measured was in 1960. It was in Chile. It hurt or killed 4,000 people. It created huge waves. The waves crossed the ocean. They hit Japan. There, they killed 170 more people.

RING OF FIRE

Most quakes occur in the Ring of Fire.
This area is in the Pacific Ocean.

The country of Chile lies
on a fault line. That's
where two underground
plates press against
each other.

The deadliest volcano is Mount Tambora. It is in Indonesia. The volcano erupted in 1815. People thousands of kilometres away heard it. The eruption killed 71,000 people.

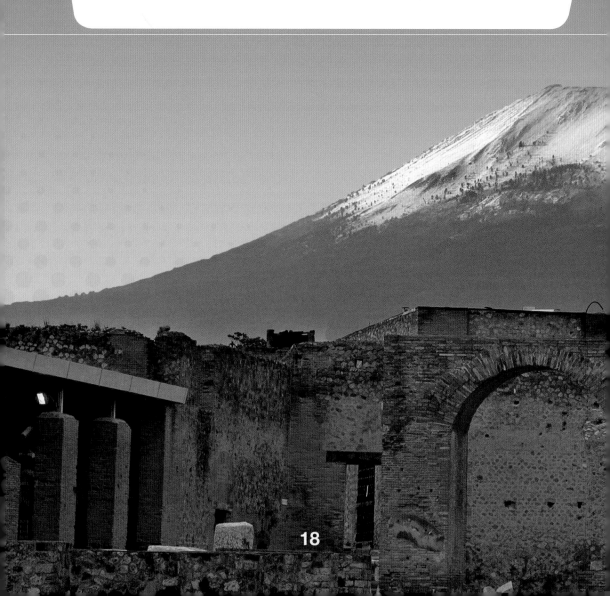

CITY DESTROYER

Italy's Mount Vesuvius erupted in AD 79. It buried a whole city. Scientists fear the volcano could erupt again. Millions of people live nearby. They could all be harmed.

People can visit the ruins of Pompeii, the city destroyed by Mount Vesuvius.

CHAPTER 5

GLOBAL
Features

Glaciers cover 10 per cent of the Earth. They hold most of the Earth's fresh water. The largest glacier is in Antarctica. It is 400 km (250 miles) long. Some of its ice is 4.7 km (3 miles) thick! Earth's sea levels would rise 64 m (210 feet) if it melted.

Glaciers around the world are melting because of rising global temperatures.

Visitors to Mammoth Cave can take guided tours through parts of the cave system.

COOL CAVES

Mammoth Cave is in Kentucky, USA. It is the longest cave system. It has more than 650 km (400 miles) of underground passages. Krubera Cave is in Eastern Europe. It is the Earth's deepest cave. The world's tallest skyscraper would fit in it 2.5 times.

The Eye of the Sahara was discovered when humans went into space.

The Eye of the Sahara is a rock. It is in the Sahara Desert. The rock is 50 km (31 miles) across! It looks like a target from above.

A rock in Australia looks like a wave. Wave Rock is 14 m (46 feet) high. It is as long as a football pitch. It is more than 2.7 billion years old!

China has a stone forest. The pillars stand tall. They have ridges. They formed over millions of years.

China's stone forest is a collection of limestone formations.

The Earth's oldest rocks are in Canada. They are in the Nuvvuagittuq Belt. The rocks are 4.28 billion years old!

The rocks in the Valley of the Moon record information from the Triassic era, which was 250 to 200 million years ago.

The Valley of the Moon is in Argentina. It looks like the Moon's surface. The site has **fossils**. Some are among Earth's oldest dinosaur fossils.

GLOSSARY

earthquake
a natural disaster in which the Earth's surface shakes

equator
an imaginary line that divides the Earth into the northern and southern hemispheres

evolve
to change over time

extinction
the dying out of an entire species

fossil
the remains of a plant or an animal that lived a long time ago

fungus
a living thing in a group that includes moulds, mildews and mushrooms

glacier
a large mass of ice and snow

magnet
a piece of iron that attracts other objects that contain iron

migration
the movement of animals from one place to another, often aligned with the seasons

orbit
to move in a set path around another object

particle
a tiny bit of something

species
a group of animals or plants that share characteristics and that can reproduce

volcano
a break in the surface of a planet that allows hot lava and ash to shoot up from inside the planet

TRIVIA

1. Antarctica is considered a desert. Its inner regions get only 5 centimetres (2 inches) of rain or snow each year.

2. The Earth's magnetic poles flip every several hundred thousand years. The North Pole used to be in Antarctica. Compasses would point towards Antarctica as north.

3. Earth's Moon has its own earthquakes. They are called moonquakes. On Earth, quakes usually stop shaking within two minutes. On the Moon, quakes can last more than 10 minutes.

ACTIVITY

MAKE A VOLCANO!

You will need:

- 1 empty plastic bottle
- modelling clay
- a funnel
- 30 grams (2 tablespoons) of bicarbonate of soda
- food colouring
- 296 ml (10 fl oz) of warm water
- a straw
- 6 drops of washing up liquid
- 60 ml (3 tablespoons) of vinegar

Check with an adult before starting this activity. Making a volcano can be messy, so find a good spot outside.

1. Place the bottle upright on the ground. Use the clay to build a mound around the bottle. Do not cover the bottle's opening. This mound will be your volcano.

2. Use the funnel to add the bicarbonate of soda to the bottle. Add a few drops of food colouring to the bottle. This will make your lava colourful.

3. Pour the water into the bottle. Fill the bottle most of the way. Remove the funnel. Use the straw to mix everything in the bottle.

4. Add the washing up liquid to the bottle. Use the straw again to mix. But this time, stir carefully. The volcano is now ready to erupt.

5. When you are ready, pour the vinegar into the bottle. Move away quickly. Watch your volcano pour out its lava!

FIND OUT MORE

Curious about the science behind these Earth facts?
Check out these resources.

Books

The Big Earth Book, Mark Brake (Lonely Planet Kids, 2017)

Planet Earth (100 Facts), Peter Riley (Miles Kelly, 2014)

Websites

DK Find Out!: Earth's Magnetic Field
www.dkfindout.com/uk/earth/structure-earth/earths-magnetic-field/

DK Find Out!: What Is a Volcano?
www.dkfindout.com/uk/earth/volcanoes/what-is-volcano/

INDEX